D1312295

# *Let's Celebrate*
# VETERANS DAY

BY Barbara deRubertis

For activities and resources for this book and
others in the HOLIDAYS & HEROES series, visit:
www.kanepress.com/holidays-and-heroes

Text copyright © 2014 by The Kane Press. Photograph/image copyrights: cover © U.S. Air Force by Maj. Dale Greer/Released; page 1 & 29 thank-you © U.S. Army by Staff Sgt. Teddy Wade/Released; 3 parade © AP Photo/Bebeto Matthews; 3 boy scout © AP Photo/Public Opinion, Markell DeLoatch; 4 army, navy, marine corps, air force © Keith McIntyre/Shutterstock; 4 coast guard © Indigoiris/Shutterstock; 5 © U.S. Marine Corps by Cpl. J. Nava/Released; 6 © U.S. Army by Staff Sgt. James Selesnick/Released; 7 helicopter interior © U.S. Army by Staff Sgt. Vince Abril/Released; 7 tank © U.S. Army by Sgt. Quentin Johnson/Released; 8 © U.S. Navy by Mass Communication Specialist Seaman Nicolas C. Lopez/Released; 9 ship © U.S. Navy by Mass Communication Specialist Seaman Nicolas C. Lopez/Released; 9 submarine © U.S. Navy by Chief Mass Communication Specialist John Lill/Released; 10 © U.S. Marine Corps by Sgt. Randall Clinton/Released; 11 tank © U.S. Marine Corps by Staff Sgt. Anthony L. Linan/Released; 11 helicopter © U.S. Marine Corps by Cpl. Ryan Carpenter/Released; 12 © U.S. Navy by Mass Communication Specialist 1st Class R. Jason Brunson/Released; 13 © Anatoliy Lukich/Shutterstock; 14 © U.S. Air Force by Staff Sgt. Larry E. Reid Jr./Released; 15 air traffic control © U.S. Air Force by Master Sgt. Carlotta Holley/Released; 15 aircraft © U.S. Air Force by Tech. Sgt. Arian Nead/Released; 16 © U.S. Army by Spc. Katherine Dowd/Released; 17 © U.S. Army by Sgt. Erica Knight/Released; 18–19 © Corbis/AP Images; 20 © Brandon Bourdages/Shutterstock; 21 © Dwight D. Eisenhower Presidential Library & Museum; 22 © Willequet Manuel/Shutterstock; 23 AF vet with poppy © AP Photo/Harry Cabluck; 23 wreath © Willequet Manuel/Shutterstock; 24 VA Medical Center © U.S. Air Force by Kemberly Groue/Released; 24 flag © David Kay/Shutterstock; 25 service dog © U.S. Marine Corps by Anthony Lazzaro/Released; 25 Warrior Games cycling © U.S. Air Force by Staff Sgt. Desiree N. Palacios/Released; 26 © Jorg Hackemann/Shutterstock; 27 © AP Photo/Manuel Balce Ceneta; 28 parade © U.S. Air Force by Maj. Dale Greer/Released; 28 WWII veterans © lev radin/Shutterstock; 29 fireworks © Nathan Guinn/Shutterstock; 29 Japanese-American WWII veterans © U.S. Air Force by Tech. Sgt. Michael R. Holzworth/Released; 30 children flag © AP Photo/Michael Orrell/El Dorado News-Times; 30 naval officer reading © U.S. Navy by Mass Communication Specialist 3rd Class Charles Oki/Released; 31 overseas care package © U.S. Air Force by Senior Airman Matt D. Schwartz/Released; 32 salute © AP Photo/Journal Star, Adam Gerik; 32 boy and veteran © AP Photo/Matt York

All due diligence has been conducted in identifying copyright holders and obtaining permissions.

Library of Congress Cataloging-in-Publication Data

deRubertis, Barbara.
 Let's celebrate Veterans Day / by Barbara deRubertis.
  pages cm. — (Holidays & heroes)
 ISBN 978-1-57565-727-1 (library binding : alk. paper) — ISBN 978-1-57565-653-3 (pbk. : alk. paper)
 1. Veterans Day—Juvenile literature. I. Title.
 D671.D48 2014
 394.264—dc23
                        2014008699
eISBN: 978-1-57565-654-0

1 3 5 7 9 10 8 6 4 2

First published in the United States of America in 2014 by Kane Press, Inc. Printed in the USA.

Book Design: Edward Miller. Photograph/Image Research: Maura Taboubi.

Visit us online at www.kanepress.com.

Like us on Facebook
facebook.com/kanepress

Follow us on Twitter
@KanePress

On November 11 of every year, Americans celebrate Veterans Day. On this day, we honor our country's veterans, the men and women who have served in the United States Armed Forces.

Cities and towns across America have parades and concerts. Schools have special assemblies. Many Americans spend time talking with family or friends who are veterans. Listening to their stories helps us appreciate all the ways they have served our country.

## Who Are Our Veterans?

Anyone who has served in one of the five branches, or parts, of the United States Armed Forces is a veteran. The five branches are:

Army

Navy

Marine Corps

Coast Guard

Air Force

Men and women can join one of these branches of the military if they are
- United States citizens or legal permanent residents,
- high school graduates,
- at least 17 years old, and
- able to pass the physical exam.

When members of the military complete their service, they are veterans. Anyone who dies or is killed while serving is also a veteran.

## The Five Branches of the Armed Forces

**The Army** is the oldest branch of the military. It was formed in June of 1775, during the early days of the American Revolution.

The Army's job is to protect the United States and its allies, or friends, on land. For example, if an enemy attacks a city, the Army will move in to defend that city and drive out the enemy.

To do this job, men and women in the Army use
- armor (such as tanks),
- air support (such as helicopters), and
- weapons (such as guns and missiles).

**The Navy** was formed just a few months after the Army, in October of 1775.

The Navy's job is to protect the right to travel freely on seas and oceans around the world. For example, if enemy ships attack, the Navy will drive away those ships or destroy them.

To do this job, the women and men in the Navy use

- ships and submarines,
- fighter aircraft and aircraft carriers, and
- weapons and missiles.

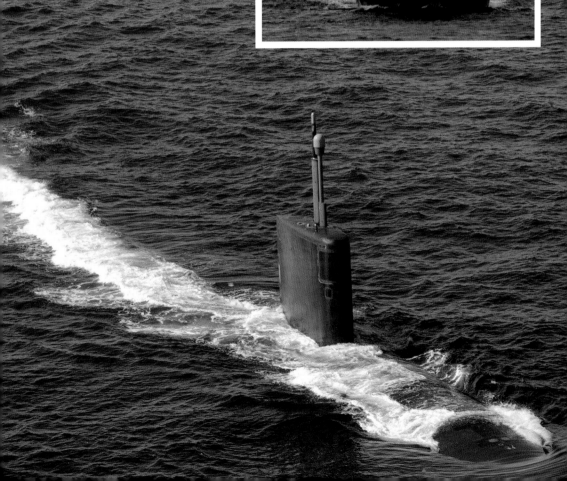

**The Marine Corps** was formed a few weeks after the Navy, in November of 1775.

The main job of the Marine Corps is to protect seacoasts. Marines also serve as fast-response teams in emergencies. For this reason, they are sometimes called "America's 9-1-1 Force." And they are experts at scouting out information about enemies.

To do all their jobs, men and women in the Marine Corps are trained to operate *everywhere*: on land, in the air, and at sea. They use special equipment that includes

- amphibious vehicles that can travel both in water and on land,
- amphibious ships that can land on enemy territory, and
- heavy-lifting helicopters for moving troops and vehicles.

**The Coast Guard** was formed in 1790. At that time it was called the Revenue Cutter Service. In 1915, it became known as the United States Coast Guard.

The main job of the Coast Guard is to offer help during emergencies in water. For example, if an airplane crashes in American waters, the Coast Guard will rush in to rescue everyone on board.

Other jobs done by the women and men of the Coast Guard include

- conducting search and rescue operations,
- enforcing laws and boating safety rules,
- protecting ports and sea travel, and
- controlling illegal activities.

To do these jobs, men and women in the Coast Guard use

- boats and ships,
- aircraft, and
- rescue stations on the shore.

The Air Force is the youngest branch of the military. It was created in 1947. Before that time, it was a part of the Army called the Army Air Corps.

The Air Force's job is to defend the United States and its friends in the air, in outer space, and in computer "cyberspace." For example, an Air Force pilot might try to stop an enemy's advance by dropping bombs on roads or bridges.

To do their jobs, women and men in the Air Force use
- fighter aircraft and bomber aircraft,
- tanker aircraft used for refueling other aircraft in the air,
- passenger and cargo aircraft,
- information-gathering aircraft, and
- helicopters.

They also use
- satellites,
- missiles, and
- computers.

## The Role of the Military in Peace and in War

**In times of peace**, members of the military must be ready to defend our country at a moment's notice. So they are always improving their skills and learning new ones.

A "stand-by" part of the military known as the National Guard is often called to help during natural disasters—such as fires, floods, and hurricanes.

**In times of war**, members of the military work together and support each other. They look out for everyone on their teams. And they always try to rescue anyone captured or injured. The unspoken rule is, "I have your back."

Most importantly, members of the military look for ways to solve both small and large problems peacefully. As many of our military leaders have said, "War is the last resort."

## Armistice Day

From 1914 to 1918, the First World War was fought. Over four million Americans served in this war. Finally, the warfare ended with an agreement to stop fighting—an armistice. People all over the world ran into the streets to celebrate when they heard the news!

Crowds in Philadelphia, PA, celebrate the armistice announcement on Nov. 11, 1918.

The armistice went into effect at the *11th hour* of the *11th day* of the *11th month*: in other words, at 11:00 in the morning on the 11th of November, 1918.

One year later, the United States celebrated the first Armistice Day on November 11, 1919. President Woodrow Wilson wanted people to honor the heroism of the Americans who had died in the war.

# Armistice Day Becomes Veterans Day

Americans had hoped that the First World War would be "the war to end all wars." But the time of peace that followed the war did not last.

From 1941 to 1945, over 16 million Americans served in the Second World War. Then, several years later, the U.S. fought again—in the Korean War.

Marine Corps War Memorial: "Raising the Flag on Iwo Jima" during the Second World War

President Dwight D. Eisenhower signs the bill that created Veterans Day in 1954.

People suggested a new idea for Armistice Day. Instead of honoring only those who had died in the First World War, the holiday should honor all veterans, living or dead. So, in 1954, Armistice Day was changed to Veterans Day.

Just like Armistice Day, Veterans Day is celebrated on November 11.

## Veterans Day, Memorial Day, and Poppies

**Veterans Day** and **Memorial Day** are both national holidays that honor members of our Armed Forces. Memorial Day specifically honors those who died while serving our country. It is celebrated on the last Monday of May.

On both holidays, many people wear red poppies. This tradition began with a poem written in 1915 by a Canadian officer, John McCrae. After he saw poppies blooming on soldiers' graves, he wrote:

*In Flanders fields the poppies blow*
*Between the crosses, row on row*
*That mark our place; and in the sky*
*The larks, still bravely singing, fly*
*Scarce heard amid the guns below....*
From "In Flanders Fields"

Flanders Field, Belgium

Red poppies soon became a symbol of the sacrifice made by those who died in the war.

Two veterans groups, the **American Legion** and the **Veterans of Foreign Wars**, began handing out poppies in the 1920s. When people receive poppies, they can give donations to help hospitalized, disabled, and needy veterans.

So if we are given poppies, we can wear them with gratitude.

## How Americans Support Veterans

Since the days of the American Revolution, the government has given special support to members of the military and their families.

**The Department of Veterans Affairs** helps veterans with many things including health care, education, job training, and loans.

If a veteran passes away, his or her family can request Military Funeral Honors. Then the **Department of Defense** will send an "honor guard" to present an American flag to the family and play "Taps."

Other groups support veterans through donations from private citizens. These groups offer many services. For example, some provide service dogs. Some provide sports equipment and training for disabled veterans.

Our veterans have sacrificed much for us. We show our gratitude by helping them in as many ways as we can.

# The Veterans Day National Ceremony

**The Veterans Day National Ceremony** is held every year at Arlington National Cemetery.

This cemetery is the home of the Tomb of the Unknowns. Three soldiers are buried here—one from the First World War, one from the Second World War, and one from the Korean War. These soldiers are "unknown" because they could not be identified when they died. They represent all American unknown soldiers.

The Tomb is guarded around the clock, every day of the year, by members of the Army. Being selected as a Tomb Guard is a high honor.

Parade of colors at the Veterans Day National Ceremony

During the Veterans Day National Ceremony, a wreath is placed at the Tomb, usually by the President of the United States. A bugler plays "Taps." Then veterans march with flags in a "parade of colors," and speeches honoring our veterans are given.

Members of the military, the families and friends of some of those buried at Arlington, and many regular American citizens attend this ceremony to show their respect for our veterans.

## Veterans Day Celebrations

Americans all across the country celebrate Veterans Day in many different ways.

People display American flags outside their homes and businesses.

Veterans march in parades through our cities and towns.

Musicians play concerts of patriotic music.
People attend "freedom festivals" and fairs.
Fireworks light up the skies.

Some restaurants offer free meals to veterans.
And lots of people wear poppies pinned to their shirts or jackets.

In schools, special Veterans Day events and programs are held. Students proudly honor family members and friends who are veterans.

We listen to our veterans tell stories about their experiences. Filming, recording, or writing down these stories makes a lasting legacy for our veterans and for us.

We can show our appreciation to active members of the military at any time of the year by writing letters, mailing packages, or simply saying "Thank you!"

Since 1775, members of the Armed Forces have had to fight in terrible wars and assist in countless disasters.

These brave men and women train their minds and bodies to be ready at a moment's notice to defend and protect us.

They love our country, our freedoms, and our people enough to risk their lives for us every day they serve in the military.

This is why we honor our veterans.

This is why we celebrate Veterans Day.